AI / ML AND THE CLOUD

UNLEASHING THE POWER OF DATA

AUTHOR

ANANT MITTAL

CONTENTS

Understanding the fundamentals of artificial intelligence (AI) and machine learning (ML) is essential in today's digital age, where these technologies are driving innovation and reshaping various industries. At its core, artificial intelligence refers to the simulation of human intelligence processes by machines, enabling them to perform tasks that typically require human cognition, such as learning, reasoning, and problem-solving. Machine learning, a subset of AI, focuses on developing algorithms and models that allow machines to learn from data and improve their performance over time without being explicitly programmed.

CHAPTER 1

INTRODUCTION TO AI AND MACHINE LEARNING

One of the key concepts in AI and ML is the notion of learning from data. Instead of relying on predefined rules or instructions, machine learning algorithms learn patterns and relationships from vast amounts of data, enabling them to make predictions, identify trends, and generate insights. This data-driven approach is central to the effectiveness of AI and ML systems, as it allows them to adapt and evolve in response to changing environments and new information.

Another fundamental aspect of AI and ML is the distinction between supervised, unsupervised, and reinforcement learning. In supervised learning, algorithms are trained on labeled datasets, where the input data is paired with corresponding output labels. The goal is to learn a mapping between inputs and outputs, allowing the algorithm to make predictions on new, unseen data. Unsupervised learning, on the other hand, involves training algorithms on unlabeled data, with the objective of discovering hidden patterns or structures within the data. Reinforcement learning is a type of learning where an agent learns to interact with an environment by taking actions and receiving feedback in the form of rewards or penalties.

Additionally, AI and ML encompass a wide range of techniques and algorithms, including neural networks, decision trees, support vector machines, and clustering algorithms, among others. These techniques can be applied to various domains and tasks, such as image recognition, natural language processing, predictive analytics, and autonomous systems.

Understanding the fundamentals of AI and ML also involves recognizing their limitations and challenges. Despite their impressive capabilities, AI and ML systems are not without biases, errors, and ethical considerations. Issues such as algorithmic bias, data privacy, and accountability require careful attention and mitigation strategies to ensure that AI technologies are developed and deployed responsibly.

In conclusion, grasping the fundamentals of artificial intelligence and machine learning is crucial for anyone interested in leveraging these technologies to drive innovation, solve complex problems, and make informed decisions. By understanding the principles, techniques, and challenges of AI and ML, individuals and organizations can harness the transformative power of these technologies to create value and positively impact society.

Exploring the role of data in driving innovation and business transformation

In today's digital age, data has emerged as a driving force behind innovation and business transformation across virtually every industry. From healthcare and finance to retail and manufacturing, organizations are leveraging the power of data to gain insights, make informed decisions, and create value for their customers and stakeholders. In this article, we'll explore the critical role of data in driving innovation and business transformation, examining how organizations are harnessing data to unlock new opportunities and stay ahead in a rapidly evolving landscape.

At the heart of data-driven innovation lies the vast amounts of data generated by individuals, devices, and systems in today's interconnected world. This data, often referred to as big data, encompasses structured and unstructured information from a variety of sources, including sensors, social media, transactions, and more. By harnessing advanced analytics and machine learning techniques, organizations can extract valuable insights from this data, uncovering patterns, trends, and correlations that were previously hidden.

One of the key ways in which data drives innovation is by enabling organizations to better understand their customers and anticipate their needs. By analyzing customer data such as purchasing behavior, preferences, and demographics, companies can tailor their products and services to meet the evolving demands of their target audience. This customer-centric approach not only enhances customer satisfaction but also fosters loyalty and retention, ultimately driving business growth and competitiveness.

Data also plays a crucial role in optimizing internal processes and operations within organizations. By leveraging data analytics and automation technologies, companies can identify inefficiencies, streamline workflows, and improve decision-making across various functions, from supply chain management and inventory optimization to marketing and sales. This data-driven approach enables organizations to reduce costs, increase productivity, and gain a competitive edge in the marketplace.

Furthermore, data fuels innovation by empowering organizations to develop new products, services, and business models that address emerging market trends and customer needs. By leveraging insights from data analysis, companies can identify gaps in the market, identify opportunities for innovation, and create disruptive solutions that differentiate them from competitors. Whether it's developing personalized healthcare solutions, launching predictive maintenance services, or implementing subscription-based business models, data-driven innovation enables organizations to stay ahead of the curve and drive growth in a rapidly evolving landscape.

Moreover, data-driven innovation has the potential to drive positive social impact and address global challenges such as climate change, healthcare disparities, and poverty. By harnessing the power of data analytics, organizations and governments can develop targeted interventions, allocate resources more efficiently, and make evidence-based policy decisions that improve the lives of individuals and communities. Whether it's predicting and mitigating the impact of natural disasters, optimizing healthcare delivery, or promoting sustainable development, data-driven innovation has the potential to create meaningful change on a global scale.

In conclusion, data plays a central role in driving innovation and business transformation in today's digital economy. By harnessing the power of data analytics, organizations can gain valuable insights, optimize processes, and develop innovative solutions that create value for customers, stakeholders, and society as a whole. As we continue to unlock the potential of data-driven innovation, the possibilities for driving positive change and shaping the future are endless.

CHAPTER 2

FOUNDATIONS OF CLOUD COMPUTING

An Overview of Cloud Computing Principles and Technologies

Cloud computing is a paradigm that enables users to access and utilize computing resources over the internet, without the need for on-premises infrastructure. At its core, cloud computing is based on several key principles:

- On-demand self-service: Users can provision computing resources, such as virtual machines, storage, and applications, on-demand without requiring human intervention from service providers.

- Scalability: Cloud services can scale dynamically to meet changing workload demands, allowing organizations to quickly scale up or down resources based on their needs.

- Pay-per-use pricing model: Cloud computing follows a pay-as-you-go pricing model, where organizations only pay for the resources they consume, eliminating the need for upfront capital investments and reducing overall IT costs.

- Resource pooling: Cloud providers aggregate computing resources across multiple users and tenants, allowing them to optimize resource utilization and achieve economies of scale.

- Rapid elasticity: Cloud services can rapidly scale resources up or down in response to changing demand, enabling organizations to handle spikes in workload without performance degradation.

Cloud computing encompasses various technologies and deployment models, including public, private, hybrid, and multi-cloud environments. Public cloud services are owned and operated by third-party providers and offer computing resources to multiple customers over the internet. Private clouds are dedicated to a single organization and can be hosted on-premises or in a third-party data center. Hybrid clouds combine public and private cloud infrastructure, while multi-cloud environments leverage multiple cloud providers to host different workloads or services.

Understanding Cloud Infrastructure, Platforms, and Services

Cloud computing offers a range of infrastructure, platforms, and services that cater to different use cases and requirements:

- Infrastructure as a Service (IaaS): IaaS provides virtualized computing resources, such as virtual machines, storage, and networking, on-demand over the internet. Customers can deploy and manage their own operating systems, applications, and middleware, while the cloud provider manages the underlying infrastructure.

- Platform as a Service (PaaS): PaaS offers a complete development and deployment environment in the cloud, including operating systems, development tools, databases, and middleware. Developers can focus on building and deploying applications without worrying about infrastructure management, scaling, or maintenance.

7

- Software as a Service (SaaS): SaaS delivers software applications over the internet on a subscription basis, eliminating the need for organizations to install, maintain, or upgrade software on their own. Examples of SaaS applications include email, collaboration tools, customer relationship management (CRM), and enterprise resource planning (ERP) software.

Cloud services can be accessed through various delivery models, including public, private, and hybrid clouds, and are available in different deployment models, such as infrastructure as a service (IaaS), platform as a service (PaaS), and software as a service (SaaS).

Benefits and Challenges of Cloud Adoption for AI and Machine Learning

The adoption of cloud computing for AI and machine learning offers several benefits, including:

- Scalability: Cloud platforms provide scalable infrastructure and resources for training and deploying machine learning models, allowing organizations to handle large-scale datasets and complex algorithms.

- Cost-effectiveness: Cloud services offer pay-as-you-go pricing models, allowing organizations to pay only for the resources they use, without the need for upfront investments in hardware or infrastructure.

- Flexibility: Cloud platforms provide a range of services and tools for AI and machine learning, allowing organizations to experiment with different algorithms, frameworks, and technologies to find the best fit for their needs.

- Collaboration: Cloud platforms enable distributed teams to collaborate on AI and machine learning projects, sharing data, models, and resources in real-time.

However, cloud adoption for AI and machine learning also presents several challenges, including:

- Data privacy and security: Storing sensitive data in the cloud raises concerns about data privacy and security, particularly in industries with strict regulatory requirements such as healthcare and finance.

- Vendor lock-in: Organizations that rely heavily on a single cloud provider may face challenges migrating their AI and machine learning workloads to another provider or on-premises infrastructure.

- Latency and performance: Latency issues can arise when training or deploying machine learning models in the cloud, particularly for real-time or latency-sensitive applications.

- Complexity: Building and managing AI and machine learning workflows in the cloud can be complex, requiring expertise in both cloud computing and data science.

In conclusion, cloud computing offers significant opportunities for organizations to leverage AI and machine learning for innovation and business transformation. However, organizations must carefully consider the benefits and challenges of cloud adoption and develop strategies to address key concerns such as data privacy, security, and performance. By leveraging the scalability, flexibility, and cost-effectiveness of cloud platforms, organizations can unlock the full potential of AI and machine learning to drive value and competitive advantage.

CHAPTER 3

CLOUD-BASED MACHINE LEARNING SERVICES

Exploring Popular Cloud-Based Machine Learning Platforms

Cloud-based machine learning platforms have become essential tools for organizations looking to leverage the power of AI and machine learning without the complexity of managing infrastructure. Here, we'll explore three popular platforms: Amazon SageMaker, Google Cloud AI Platform, and Microsoft Azure Machine Learning.

1. Amazon SageMaker:

Amazon SageMaker is a fully managed service that provides developers and data scientists with the tools to build, train, and deploy machine learning models at scale. It offers a range of features, including:

- Data preparation and exploration: SageMaker provides built-in tools for data preprocessing, visualization, and analysis, making it easy to prepare and explore datasets.

- Model training: SageMaker supports a variety of machine learning algorithms and frameworks, including TensorFlow, PyTorch, and Scikit-learn, allowing users to train models using their preferred tools.

- Model hosting and deployment: Once trained, models can be deployed to SageMaker endpoints for real-time inference, or batch transform jobs for offline predictions.

- AutoML capabilities: SageMaker Autopilot automates the machine learning pipeline, from data preprocessing to model selection and tuning, making it easier to build high-quality models with minimal effort.

2. Google Cloud AI Platform:

Google Cloud AI Platform is a suite of cloud-based machine learning services that enables developers and data scientists to build, train, and deploy models on Google Cloud. Key features include:

- Integrated development environment: AI Platform Notebooks provides a collaborative environment for developing machine learning models using Jupyter notebooks.

- Managed training and hyperparameter tuning: AI Platform Training allows users to train models at scale using distributed training, and automatically tunes hyperparameters to optimize model performance.

- Model serving and deployment: AI Platform Prediction enables users to deploy trained models as RESTful APIs for online prediction, or as batch prediction jobs for offline inference.

- Pre-built models and APIs: AI Platform offers a range of pre-trained models and APIs for common tasks such as image recognition, speech-to-text, and translation, making it easy to incorporate AI capabilities into applications.

3. Microsoft Azure Machine Learning:

Azure Machine Learning is a comprehensive machine learning service that enables organizations to build, train, and deploy models on Microsoft Azure. Key features include:

- Visual interface and drag-and-drop workflow: Azure Machine Learning Studio provides a visual interface for building and deploying machine learning models, allowing users to create workflows using a drag-and-drop interface.

- Automated machine learning: Azure AutoML automates the process of model selection, feature engineering, and hyperparameter tuning, making it easier to build high-quality models with minimal manual intervention.

- Model deployment and management: Azure Machine Learning enables users to deploy models to Azure Kubernetes Service (AKS) for scalable, high-performance inference, and provides tools for monitoring and managing deployed models.

- Integration with Azure services: Azure Machine Learning integrates seamlessly with other Azure services, such as Azure Databricks for data processing and Azure DevOps for model lifecycle management, providing a complete end-to-end solution for machine learning.

Overall, these cloud-based machine learning platforms offer powerful tools and capabilities for organizations to build, train, and deploy machine learning models at scale. Whether you're a developer, data scientist, or business user, these platforms provide the tools and infrastructure needed to unlock the full potential of AI and machine learning in the cloud.

Leveraging Pre-built Models, Algorithms, and Tools for Training, Deployment, and Management of Machine Learning Models in the Cloud

The availability of pre-built models, algorithms, and tools for training, deployment, and management of machine learning models in the cloud has significantly simplified the development process and accelerated the adoption of AI technologies. Here, we'll explore how organizations can leverage these resources to build and deploy machine learning models more efficiently.

1. Pre-built models:

Many cloud providers offer pre-trained models for common machine learning tasks, such as image recognition, natural language processing, and speech recognition. These models are trained on large datasets and can be easily integrated into applications using APIs or SDKs provided by the cloud platform. By leveraging pre-built models, organizations can quickly add AI capabilities to their applications without the need to train models from scratch.

2. Algorithms and libraries:

Cloud-based machine learning platforms provide access to a wide range of algorithms and libraries for training and deploying machine learning models. These libraries, such as TensorFlow, PyTorch, and Scikit-learn, offer implementations of popular algorithms and techniques for tasks such as classification, regression, clustering, and more. By leveraging these libraries, data scientists and developers can quickly prototype and experiment with different models and techniques, accelerating the development process.

3. AutoML tools:

AutoML (automated machine learning) tools automate the process of model selection, feature engineering, and hyperparameter tuning, making it easier to build high-quality models with minimal manual intervention. These tools, such as Google Cloud AutoML, Azure AutoML, and Amazon SageMaker Autopilot, enable organizations to quickly build and deploy machine learning models without requiring deep expertise in machine learning algorithms and techniques.

4. Model deployment and management:

Cloud-based machine learning platforms offer tools and services for deploying and managing machine learning models in production environments. These services, such as Amazon SageMaker, Google Cloud AI Platform, and Microsoft Azure Machine Learning, provide capabilities for deploying models as RESTful APIs, monitoring model performance, and managing model versions. By leveraging these services, organizations can ensure that their machine learning models are deployed securely, scalable, and reliable.

In conclusion, the availability of pre-built models, algorithms, and tools for training, deployment, and management of machine learning models in the cloud has democratized access to AI technologies and accelerated the adoption of machine learning in various industries. By leveraging these resources, organizations can build and deploy machine learning models more efficiently, enabling them to unlock the full potential of AI and drive innovation in their business.

CHAPTER 4

DATA MANAGEMENT AND STORAGE IN THE CLOUD

Best Practices for Managing and Storing Large Datasets in the Cloud

Managing and storing large datasets in the cloud requires careful planning, optimization, and adherence to best practices to ensure efficient performance, scalability, and cost-effectiveness. Here are some best practices to consider:

- Data Partitioning: Partitioning large datasets into smaller, manageable chunks can improve query performance and reduce latency. By distributing data across multiple partitions based on key attributes such as date, region, or customer ID, organizations can parallelize data processing and optimize resource utilization.

- Compression: Utilizing compression techniques can reduce storage costs and improve data transfer speeds by compressing large datasets before storing them in the cloud. However, it's essential to strike a balance between compression efficiency and computational overhead to avoid compromising performance.

- Data Lifecycle Management: Implementing data lifecycle policies can help organizations manage data retention, archival, and deletion effectively. By defining rules and policies based on data access frequency, age, or business relevance, organizations can optimize storage costs and ensure compliance with regulatory requirements.

- Data Encryption: Encrypting data at rest and in transit is essential for protecting sensitive information and maintaining data security in the cloud. Utilizing encryption techniques such as AES encryption and SSL/TLS encryption can safeguard data against unauthorized access and data breaches.

- Backup and Disaster Recovery: Implementing backup and disaster recovery strategies is crucial for ensuring data availability and resilience in the event of data loss or system failures. Organizations should regularly back up their data to geographically distributed locations and test their disaster recovery plans to ensure they can quickly recover from potential outages.

- Monitoring and Performance Tuning: Monitoring data storage and performance metrics can help organizations identify bottlenecks, optimize resource utilization, and proactively address issues before they impact operations. Utilizing cloud-native monitoring tools and performance tuning techniques can help organizations optimize data storage and improve overall system performance.

- Compliance and Governance: Ensuring compliance with regulatory requirements and industry standards is essential when managing and storing large datasets in the cloud. Organizations should implement robust access controls, audit trails, and data governance policies to protect sensitive information and maintain regulatory compliance.

- Cost Optimization: Optimizing costs is a critical consideration when managing large datasets in the cloud. By leveraging cost management tools, reserved instances, and spot instances, organizations can optimize their cloud spending and minimize unnecessary expenses associated with data storage and processing.

Exploring Cloud-Native Data Storage Solutions

Cloud-native data storage solutions offer scalable, reliable, and cost-effective options for storing and managing large datasets in the cloud. Here are some popular cloud-native data storage solutions offered by leading cloud providers:

- Amazon S3 (Simple Storage Service): Amazon S3 is a highly scalable object storage service offered by Amazon Web Services (AWS). It provides durable and reliable storage for a wide range of use cases, including data lakes, backup and archiving, content distribution, and analytics. With features such as versioning, lifecycle management, and encryption, Amazon S3 is a versatile solution for storing large datasets in the cloud.

- Google Cloud Storage: Google Cloud Storage is a fully managed object storage service provided by Google Cloud Platform (GCP). It offers scalable and durable storage for a variety of data types, including structured and unstructured data. With features such as regional and multi-regional storage, lifecycle management, and access controls, Google Cloud Storage is well-suited for storing large datasets and powering data-intensive applications.

- Azure Data Lake Storage: Azure Data Lake Storage is a scalable and secure data lake solution offered by Microsoft Azure. It provides a unified storage platform for storing structured and unstructured data, enabling organizations to analyze and process large datasets with ease. With features such as hierarchical namespace, fine-grained access controls, and integration with Azure services, Azure Data Lake Storage is ideal for building data lakes and implementing big data analytics solutions.

Strategies for Data Preprocessing, Transformation, and Cleaning in the Cloud Environment

Data preprocessing, transformation, and cleaning are essential steps in the data analytics pipeline, enabling organizations to prepare and wrangle raw data into a usable format for analysis and insights. In the cloud environment, several strategies can help organizations streamline and optimize these processes:

- Parallel Processing: Leveraging cloud-native distributed computing frameworks such as Apache Spark, Hadoop, and Apache Flink can enable organizations to parallelize data preprocessing and transformation tasks, reducing processing times and improving efficiency.

- Serverless Computing: Utilizing serverless computing platforms such as AWS Lambda, Google Cloud Functions, and Azure Functions can enable organizations to run data preprocessing and transformation tasks without provisioning or managing infrastructure. Serverless computing offers scalability, flexibility, and cost-effectiveness, as organizations only pay for the compute resources consumed during execution.

- Managed Data Services: Leveraging managed data services such as AWS Glue, Google Cloud Dataflow, and Azure Data Factory can simplify data preprocessing and transformation tasks by providing pre-built connectors, data pipelines, and transformation capabilities. Managed data services offer automation, scalability, and integration with cloud-native data storage solutions, enabling organizations to streamline data processing workflows.

- Data Quality Monitoring: Implementing data quality monitoring tools and techniques can help organizations identify and address data quality issues during preprocessing and transformation. By establishing data quality metrics, thresholds, and alerts, organizations can ensure that data meets predefined standards and requirements before analysis and insights generation.

- Data Lineage and Governance: Establishing data lineage and governance processes can help organizations track the origin, usage, and transformation of data throughout the data lifecycle. By documenting data lineage, organizations can ensure data integrity, compliance, and accountability, enabling stakeholders to trust and verify the validity of analytical results.

- Automated Data Cleansing: Leveraging automated data cleansing tools and techniques can help organizations identify and rectify errors, inconsistencies, and outliers in the data. By implementing data validation rules, data profiling, and anomaly detection algorithms, organizations can improve data quality and accuracy, reducing the risk of errors and biases in analytical results.

In conclusion, managing and storing large datasets in the cloud requires organizations to implement best practices, leverage cloud-native data storage solutions, and adopt strategies for data preprocessing, transformation, and cleaning. By following these guidelines, organizations can optimize performance, scalability, and cost-effectiveness, enabling them to derive valuable insights and unlock the full potential of their data assets in the cloud environment.

CHAPTER 5

SCALABLE COMPUTING AND PROCESSING

Harnessing the Power of Cloud Computing for Scalable Data Processing and Analysis

Cloud computing offers unparalleled scalability and flexibility for data processing and analysis, enabling organizations to efficiently manage and analyze vast amounts of data. By leveraging cloud-based infrastructure and services, organizations can overcome traditional limitations associated with on-premises data processing, such as hardware constraints, scalability issues, and infrastructure maintenance costs.

One of the key advantages of cloud computing for data processing is its ability to dynamically scale resources based on workload demands. Cloud providers offer scalable computing resources, such as virtual machines and containers, that can be provisioned and decommissioned on-demand, allowing organizations to efficiently handle fluctuating workloads without overprovisioning resources.

Additionally, cloud computing provides a wide range of data processing and analysis tools and services that are designed to streamline workflows and improve productivity. These include managed big data services such as Amazon EMR, Google Dataproc, and Azure HDInsight, which offer pre-configured clusters and integrated tools for running distributed data processing frameworks like Apache Spark and Hadoop.

Furthermore, cloud-based data processing and analysis enable organizations to leverage advanced analytics and machine learning algorithms to extract valuable insights from their data. By integrating machine learning models with cloud-based data processing pipelines, organizations can automate data analysis tasks, identify patterns and trends, and make data-driven decisions in real-time.

In conclusion, cloud computing provides organizations with a powerful platform for scalable data processing and analysis, enabling them to efficiently manage and analyze large volumes of data. By leveraging cloud-based infrastructure and services, organizations can overcome traditional limitations associated with on-premises data processing and unlock new opportunities for innovation and growth.

Understanding Distributed Computing Frameworks such as Apache Spark and Hadoop in the Cloud

Distributed computing frameworks such as Apache Spark and Hadoop play a critical role in enabling scalable and efficient data processing in the cloud. These frameworks are designed to distribute data processing tasks across multiple nodes or machines, allowing organizations to parallelize computations and handle large datasets with ease.

Apache Spark is a fast and general-purpose distributed computing framework that is widely used for big data processing and analysis. It provides a rich set of APIs and libraries for building complex data processing pipelines, including support for batch processing, stream processing, machine learning, and graph processing. Spark's in-memory processing capabilities and fault tolerance mechanisms make it well-suited for processing large-scale datasets in the cloud.

Hadoop is another popular distributed computing framework that is commonly used for storing and processing big data. It consists of two main components: the Hadoop Distributed File System (HDFS) for distributed storage and the MapReduce programming model for distributed processing. Hadoop's distributed storage architecture and fault tolerance mechanisms make it ideal for storing and processing large volumes of data in the cloud.

In addition to Apache Spark and Hadoop, there are several other distributed computing frameworks and technologies that are commonly used in the cloud, including Apache Flink, Apache Kafka, and Google Dataflow. These frameworks offer unique features and capabilities for processing and analyzing data in real-time, enabling organizations to build scalable and efficient data processing pipelines in the cloud.

Overall, distributed computing frameworks such as Apache Spark and Hadoop play a critical role in enabling scalable and efficient data processing in the cloud. By leveraging these frameworks, organizations can parallelize computations, handle large datasets with ease, and unlock new opportunities for innovation and growth.

Optimizing Performance and Cost-effectiveness through Cloud-based Parallel Processing and Distributed Computing

Cloud-based parallel processing and distributed computing offer organizations the opportunity to optimize performance and cost-effectiveness when processing large volumes of data. By distributing data processing tasks across multiple nodes or machines, organizations can parallelize computations, reduce processing times, and improve overall performance.

One of the key benefits of cloud-based parallel processing is its ability to scale resources dynamically based on workload demands. Cloud providers offer scalable computing resources, such as virtual machines and containers, that can be provisioned and decommissioned on-demand, allowing organizations to efficiently handle fluctuating workloads without overprovisioning resources.

Additionally, cloud-based parallel processing enables organizations to leverage cost-effective pricing models for compute resources. Cloud providers offer pay-as-you-go pricing models, where organizations only pay for the resources they consume, eliminating the need for upfront capital investments in hardware or infrastructure. By optimizing resource utilization and scaling resources based on workload demands, organizations can minimize costs while maximizing performance.

Furthermore, cloud-based parallel processing enables organizations to leverage advanced analytics and machine learning algorithms to extract valuable insights from their data. By parallelizing computations and distributing data processing tasks across multiple nodes or machines, organizations can accelerate the time-to-insight and make data-driven decisions in real-time.

In conclusion, cloud-based parallel processing and distributed computing offer organizations the opportunity to optimize performance and cost-effectiveness when processing large volumes of data. By parallelizing computations, scaling resources dynamically, and leveraging cost-effective pricing models, organizations can efficiently handle fluctuating workloads, minimize costs, and unlock new opportunities for innovation and growth.

CHAPTER 6

AI MODEL TRAINING AND OPTIMIZATION

Techniques for Training and Optimizing Machine Learning Models in the Cloud

Training and optimizing machine learning models in the cloud involves leveraging cloud-based infrastructure, tools, and techniques to maximize performance, scalability, and efficiency. Several techniques can be employed for this purpose:

- Distributed Training: Cloud platforms offer distributed computing capabilities that allow training large-scale machine learning models across multiple nodes or instances in parallel. Distributed training techniques such as data parallelism and model parallelism enable faster convergence and scalability by distributing the computational workload.

- AutoML: Automated machine learning (AutoML) tools and platforms available in the cloud automate the process of model selection, feature engineering, and hyperparameter tuning. AutoML algorithms use techniques such as genetic algorithms, Bayesian optimization, and neural architecture search to search for the best-performing machine learning model and hyperparameters.

- Transfer Learning: Transfer learning is a technique where a pre-trained model is fine-tuned on a specific task or dataset to achieve better performance. Cloud-based machine learning platforms often provide access to pre-trained models and transfer learning frameworks, enabling organizations to leverage existing knowledge and expertise to accelerate model training and optimization.

- Model Compression: Model compression techniques such as pruning, quantization, and knowledge distillation reduce the size and computational complexity of machine learning models, making them more efficient to deploy and run in cloud environments. By compressing models, organizations can reduce inference latency, memory footprint, and energy consumption without sacrificing performance.

- Ensemble Learning: Ensemble learning techniques combine multiple machine learning models to improve predictive accuracy and robustness. Cloud-based machine learning platforms offer tools and libraries for building, training, and deploying ensemble models, such as random forests, gradient boosting, and neural network ensembles.

Leveraging Cloud-Based Resources for Hyperparameter Tuning, Model Selection, and Optimization

Hyperparameter tuning, model selection, and optimization are critical steps in the machine learning workflow that can significantly impact model performance and effectiveness. Cloud-based resources offer several advantages for conducting hyperparameter tuning, model selection, and optimization:

- Scalability: Cloud platforms provide access to scalable computing resources, enabling organizations to conduct large-scale hyperparameter tuning experiments across multiple instances or nodes in parallel. By leveraging cloud-based infrastructure, organizations can accelerate the optimization process and explore a wider range of hyperparameter configurations.

- Automation: Cloud-based machine learning platforms offer automated tools and services for hyperparameter tuning, such as AWS SageMaker's automatic model tuning or Google Cloud AI Platform's hyperparameter tuning service. These services automate the process of searching for the optimal hyperparameter values, allowing organizations to focus on model development and experimentation rather than manual tuning.

- Experiment Tracking: Cloud-based machine learning platforms often include features for tracking and managing hyperparameter tuning experiments, such as tracking hyperparameter configurations, model performance metrics, and experiment outcomes. By centralizing experiment tracking in the cloud, organizations can gain insights into the effectiveness of different hyperparameter configurations and make informed decisions about model selection and optimization.

- Cost-Effectiveness: Cloud platforms offer flexible pricing models that allow organizations to pay only for the resources they use, making hyperparameter tuning and optimization cost-effective. By leveraging cloud-based resources for hyperparameter tuning, organizations can avoid the upfront costs associated with provisioning on-premises infrastructure and scale resources up or down based on demand.

- Integration with ML Frameworks: Cloud-based machine learning platforms provide integration with popular machine learning frameworks and libraries, such as TensorFlow, PyTorch, and scikit-learn, making it easy to conduct hyperparameter tuning and optimization using familiar tools and workflows.

Strategies for Managing Model Versioning, Experimentation, and Reproducibility in the Cloud Environment

Managing model versioning, experimentation, and reproducibility is essential for ensuring the integrity, transparency, and reliability of machine learning workflows in the cloud environment. Several strategies can be employed to achieve these objectives:

- Version Control: Adopting version control systems such as Git or GitLab for managing machine learning code, scripts, and configurations. By using version control, organizations can track changes to machine learning models, collaborate with team members, and maintain a history of experiments and iterations.

- Experiment Tracking: Leveraging experiment tracking tools and platforms such as MLflow, TensorBoard, or Neptune.ai for logging hyperparameter configurations, model performance metrics, and experiment outcomes. These tools provide visibility into the experimentation process, enabling organizations to analyze results, compare experiments, and make data-driven decisions about model development and optimization.

- Containerization: Using containerization technologies such as Docker or Kubernetes to package machine learning code, dependencies, and environments into portable and reproducible containers. By containerizing machine learning workflows, organizations can ensure consistency across development, testing, and production environments, and facilitate deployment and scaling in the cloud.

- Artifact Management: Implementing artifact management systems or platforms such as DVC (Data Version Control) or MLflow for tracking and managing machine learning artifacts, such as trained models, datasets, and evaluation metrics. These systems provide a centralized repository for storing and versioning artifacts, enabling organizations to reproduce experiments, reproduce results, and share findings with stakeholders.

- Documentation and Collaboration: Establishing documentation and collaboration practices to document machine learning experiments, methodologies, and findings, and facilitate knowledge sharing and collaboration among team members. By documenting experiments and workflows, organizations can ensure transparency, reproducibility, and accountability in the machine learning process.

In conclusion, cloud computing offers organizations a range of tools, technologies, and capabilities for training, optimizing, and managing machine learning models at scale. By leveraging cloud-based resources for hyperparameter tuning, model selection, and optimization, organizations can accelerate the machine learning workflow, achieve better performance, and drive innovation.

Additionally, adopting strategies for managing model versioning, experimentation, and reproducibility in the cloud environment ensures the integrity, transparency, and reliability of machine learning workflows, enabling organizations to make informed decisions and derive actionable insights from their data.

CHAPTER 7

DEPLOYMENT AND SERVING OF AI MODELS

Best Practices for Deploying and Serving Machine Learning Models in the Cloud

Deploying and serving machine learning models in the cloud requires careful planning and execution to ensure optimal performance, scalability, and reliability. Here are some best practices to consider:

- Containerization: Containerization enables you to package your machine learning models and their dependencies into lightweight, portable containers. This allows for consistent deployment across different environments and facilitates scalability and version control.

- Microservices Architecture: Adopting a microservices architecture allows you to break down your machine learning application into smaller, independent services, each responsible for a specific task or functionality. This improves scalability, fault isolation, and maintainability.

- Version Control: Implement version control for your machine learning models to track changes, experiment with different versions, and roll back to previous versions if necessary. This ensures reproducibility and enables collaboration among team members.

- Continuous Integration and Deployment (CI/CD): Implement CI/CD pipelines to automate the process of building, testing, and deploying machine learning models in the cloud. This streamlines development workflows, reduces manual errors, and accelerates time-to-market.

- Scalability: Design your machine learning infrastructure to scale dynamically based on workload demands. Use auto-scaling capabilities offered by cloud providers to automatically adjust computing resources up or down in response to changes in traffic or demand.

- Monitoring and Alerting: Implement robust monitoring and alerting systems to track the performance, health, and availability of deployed machine learning models. Monitor key metrics such as latency, throughput, error rates, and resource utilization, and set up alerts to notify you of any anomalies or issues.

- Security: Ensure that your machine learning infrastructure is secure by implementing encryption, access controls, and authentication mechanisms. Follow best practices for securing data at rest and in transit, and regularly audit and review your security controls to identify and mitigate potential vulnerabilities.

- Cost Optimization: Optimize costs by right-sizing your computing resources, leveraging spot instances or preemptible VMs for non-critical workloads, and implementing cost monitoring and management tools provided by cloud providers.

- Fault Tolerance: Design your machine learning infrastructure to be resilient to failures by implementing redundancy, failover mechanisms, and disaster recovery strategies. Use load balancing and distributed architectures to ensure high availability and reliability.

- Documentation and Knowledge Sharing: Document your deployment process, configuration settings, and operational procedures to facilitate knowledge sharing and collaboration among team members. This helps onboard new team members and ensures consistency and reproducibility in deployment practices.

By following these best practices, you can ensure that your machine learning models are deployed and served in the cloud in a scalable, reliable, and cost-effective manner, enabling you to unlock the full potential of your AI applications.

Exploring Containerization and Serverless Computing for Scalable and Cost-Effective Model Deployment

Containerization and serverless computing have emerged as popular approaches for deploying and serving machine learning models in the cloud, offering scalability, flexibility, and cost-effectiveness. Here's how you can leverage these technologies for model deployment:

- Containerization: Containerization enables you to package your machine learning models, dependencies, and runtime environment into lightweight, portable containers. This allows for consistent deployment across different environments and platforms, simplifies dependency management, and facilitates scalability and version control.

- Docker and Kubernetes: Docker is a popular containerization platform that allows you to build, ship, and run containers on any infrastructure. Kubernetes is an open-source container orchestration platform that automates the deployment, scaling, and management of containerized applications. Together, Docker and Kubernetes provide a powerful solution for deploying and managing machine learning models at scale.

- Serverless Computing: Serverless computing, also known as Function as a Service (FaaS), allows you to run code in response to events without provisioning or managing servers. This eliminates the need to manage infrastructure and enables you to focus on writing and deploying code. Serverless platforms such as AWS Lambda, Google Cloud Functions, and Azure Functions provide a scalable and cost-effective solution for deploying machine learning models.

- Event-Driven Architecture: Serverless computing is well-suited for event-driven architectures, where machine learning models are invoked in response to events such as HTTP requests, messages from message queues, or changes in data streams. This enables you to build reactive and scalable applications that respond dynamically to changes in the environment.

- Cost Optimization: Serverless computing offers a pay-per-use pricing model, where you only pay for the compute resources consumed by your functions. This can result in cost savings compared to traditional server-based deployments, especially for applications with variable or unpredictable workloads.

- Cold Start Latency: One challenge of serverless computing is cold start latency, where there is a delay in response time when a function is invoked for the first time or after a period of inactivity. To mitigate cold start latency, you can use techniques such as pre-warming, where functions are invoked periodically to keep them warm and ready to respond quickly.

- Integration with Cloud Services: Serverless platforms integrate seamlessly with other cloud services, such as storage, databases, and messaging, enabling you to build end-to-end machine learning applications that leverage the full capabilities of the cloud.

By leveraging containerization and serverless computing, you can deploy and serve machine learning models in a scalable, cost-effective, and flexible manner, enabling you to build and deploy AI applications that meet the demands of modern business environments.

Strategies for Monitoring, Logging, and Managing Deployed Models in Production Environments

Monitoring, logging, and managing deployed machine learning models in production environments is crucial for ensuring their reliability, performance, and scalability. Here are some strategies to consider:

- Real-Time Monitoring: Implement real-time monitoring of deployed models to track key performance metrics such as latency, throughput, error rates, and resource utilization. Use monitoring tools and dashboards to visualize and analyze these metrics, and set up alerts to notify you of any anomalies or performance degradation.

- Logging and Auditing: Implement logging and auditing mechanisms to record important events, errors, and user interactions related to deployed models. Log model predictions, input data, and output responses to facilitate troubleshooting, debugging, and auditing of model behavior.

- Model Versioning: Implement version control for deployed models to track changes, experiment with different versions, and roll back to previous versions if necessary. This ensures reproducibility and enables you to compare the performance of different model versions over time.

- A/B Testing: Conduct A/B testing or experiments to evaluate the performance of different model versions or configurations in production. Compare metrics such as accuracy, precision, recall, and user engagement to determine the impact of changes on model performance and user experience.

- Feedback Loops: Implement feedback loops to continuously collect data and user feedback from deployed models, and use this information to retrain and improve model performance over time. Monitor model drift and concept drift to detect changes in data distributions or user behavior that may impact model performance.

- Security and Compliance: Ensure that deployed models comply with security and privacy regulations by implementing encryption, access controls, and authentication mechanisms. Follow best practices for securing data at rest and in transit, and regularly audit and review your security controls to identify and mitigate potential vulnerabilities.

- Scalability and Resource Management: Monitor resource utilization and performance of deployed models to ensure optimal scalability and resource efficiency. Use auto-scaling capabilities offered by cloud providers to automatically adjust computing resources up or down in response to changes in workload demands.

- Incident Response and Recovery: Develop incident response and recovery plans to quickly address and mitigate any issues or failures that may occur in production. Establish communication channels, escalation procedures, and incident response playbooks to ensure a coordinated and timely response to incidents.

By implementing these strategies, you can effectively monitor, log, and manage deployed machine learning models in production environments, ensuring their reliability, performance, and scalability, and maximizing their value to your organization.

CHAPTER 8

REAL-WORLD APPLICATIONS AND USE CASES

A rtificial intelligence (AI) and machine learning (ML) technologies are revolutionizing various industries, driving innovation, and unlocking new opportunities for organizations. Some of the real-world applications and use cases of AI and ML include:

Healthcare:

- Medical Imaging: AI algorithms are used to analyze medical images such as X-rays, MRIs, and CT scans to detect abnormalities, tumors, and other medical conditions with higher accuracy and efficiency than traditional methods.

- Drug Discovery: ML techniques are employed to analyze large datasets of molecular structures, genetic information, and clinical trial data to identify potential drug candidates, predict drug interactions, and accelerate the drug discovery process.

- Personalized Medicine: AI-driven algorithms are used to analyze patient data, including genetic information, medical history, and lifestyle factors, to develop personalized treatment plans and interventions tailored to individual patients' needs.

Finance:

- Fraud Detection: ML algorithms are used to analyze transactional data and detect fraudulent activities, such as credit card fraud, identity theft, and money laundering, in real-time, helping financial institutions prevent financial losses and protect their customers.

- Risk Management: AI models are employed to assess credit risk, market risk, and operational risk by analyzing historical data, market trends, and macroeconomic indicators, enabling financial institutions to make informed decisions and mitigate risks.

- Algorithmic Trading: ML algorithms are used to analyze financial markets, identify trading patterns, and execute trades automatically based on predefined rules and strategies, helping investors optimize their investment portfolios and maximize returns.

Retail:

- Customer Segmentation: AI-driven algorithms are used to analyze customer data, including purchase history, browsing behavior, and demographic information, to segment customers into different groups and target them with personalized marketing campaigns and recommendations.

- Demand Forecasting: ML models are employed to analyze sales data, market trends, and external factors such as weather and holidays to predict future demand for products and optimize inventory management and supply chain operations.

- Dynamic Pricing: AI algorithms are used to adjust product prices in real-time based on factors such as demand, competitor pricing, and customer behavior, helping retailers maximize profits and improve sales margins.

Manufacturing:

- Predictive Maintenance: ML models are used to analyze sensor data from machinery and equipment to predict equipment failures, identify maintenance needs, and schedule maintenance activities proactively, reducing downtime and increasing operational efficiency.

- Quality Control: AI-driven algorithms are employed to inspect and analyze product defects, anomalies, and imperfections in manufacturing processes, ensuring product quality and minimizing defects and recalls.

- Supply Chain Optimization: ML techniques are used to optimize supply chain operations, including inventory management, logistics, and distribution, by analyzing data from multiple sources, identifying inefficiencies, and optimizing processes to reduce costs and improve delivery times.

Case Studies and Examples of AI and Machine Learning Applications

- Healthcare: IBM Watson Health uses AI and ML algorithms to analyze medical data and provide insights for personalized treatment plans, disease diagnosis, and drug discovery.

- Finance: JPMorgan Chase uses AI-driven algorithms to analyze market data and optimize trading strategies, enabling traders to make faster and more informed decisions.

- Retail: Amazon uses machine learning algorithms to power its recommendation engine, providing personalized product recommendations to customers based on their browsing and purchase history.

- Manufacturing: General Electric uses AI and ML techniques to optimize maintenance schedules for its aircraft engines, reducing downtime and maintenance costs.

Insights into How Organizations are Leveraging Cloud Computing for AI and Machine Learning

Organizations are increasingly leveraging cloud computing to drive innovation and gain a competitive advantage through AI and machine learning. Some insights into how organizations are leveraging cloud computing for AI and machine learning include:

- Scalability: Cloud computing provides organizations with scalable infrastructure and resources for training and deploying machine learning models, enabling them to handle large-scale datasets and complex algorithms with ease.

- Cost-effectiveness: Cloud platforms offer pay-as-you-go pricing models, allowing organizations to pay only for the resources they use, without the need for upfront investments in hardware or infrastructure.

- Flexibility: Cloud platforms provide a range of services and tools for AI and machine learning, allowing organizations to experiment with different algorithms, frameworks, and technologies to find the best fit for their needs.

- Collaboration: Cloud platforms enable distributed teams to collaborate on AI and machine learning projects, sharing data, models, and resources in real-time.

Overall, cloud computing provides organizations with the scalability, flexibility, and cost-effectiveness needed to harness the power of AI and machine learning and drive innovation and competitive advantage in today's digital economy.

CHAPTER 9

SECURITY, PRIVACY, AND COMPLIANCE

Addressing Security, Privacy, and Compliance Considerations in Cloud-based AI and Machine Learning Environments

As organizations increasingly leverage cloud-based AI and machine learning (ML) environments, addressing security, privacy, and compliance considerations becomes paramount. These environments often deal with sensitive data and require robust measures to protect against security threats and ensure compliance with regulations.

To address security concerns, organizations should implement encryption techniques to protect data both at rest and in transit. Additionally, access control mechanisms should be enforced to limit access to sensitive data and resources only to authorized users. Regular security audits and vulnerability assessments can help identify and mitigate potential security risks.

Privacy considerations are equally important, especially when dealing with personal or sensitive information. Organizations should adhere to privacy best practices, such as data anonymization and minimization, to protect user privacy. Transparent data handling practices, including clear privacy policies and consent mechanisms, help build trust with users and demonstrate a commitment to protecting their privacy.

Compliance with regulations such as GDPR, HIPAA, and PCI-DSS is essential for organizations operating in cloud-based AI and ML environments. These regulations impose strict requirements for data protection, privacy, and security, and non-compliance can result in severe penalties and reputational damage. Organizations must ensure that their cloud-based AI and ML solutions comply with relevant regulations by implementing appropriate controls, policies, and procedures.

Strategies for Securing Data, Models, and Infrastructure in the Cloud

Securing data, models, and infrastructure in cloud-based AI and ML environments requires a multi-layered approach that addresses various security threats and vulnerabilities.

- Data Security: Implement encryption techniques to protect data both at rest and in transit. Use access control mechanisms to limit access to sensitive data and monitor data access and usage. Regularly audit data access logs to detect and mitigate unauthorized access attempts.

- Model Security: Secure machine learning models by implementing robust authentication and authorization mechanisms. Protect model training data and parameters from unauthorized access or modification. Implement version control and monitoring mechanisms to track changes to models and detect potential security breaches.

- Infrastructure Security: Secure cloud infrastructure by implementing strong authentication and access control measures. Regularly patch and update software to address known vulnerabilities. Implement network segmentation and firewall rules to protect against unauthorized access and network attacks.

Compliance with Regulations such as GDPR, HIPAA, and PCI-DSS in the Context of AI and Machine Learning

Compliance with regulations such as GDPR, HIPAA, and PCI-DSS is critical for organizations operating in cloud-based AI and machine learning environments. These regulations impose strict requirements for data protection, privacy, and security, and non-compliance can result in severe penalties and reputational damage.

To ensure compliance with regulations:

- GDPR Compliance: Implement measures to protect personal data, such as encryption, access controls, and data anonymization. Obtain explicit consent from users before collecting and processing their personal data. Implement data protection impact assessments (DPIAs) to identify and mitigate privacy risks associated with AI and ML processes.

- HIPAA Compliance: Implement safeguards to protect the confidentiality, integrity, and availability of protected health information (PHI). Implement access controls, audit trails, and encryption to secure PHI. Implement policies and procedures to ensure the secure transmission and storage of PHI in cloud-based AI and ML environments.

- PCI-DSS Compliance: Implement measures to protect payment card data, such as encryption, tokenization, and access controls. Ensure that cloud service providers comply with PCI-DSS requirements and obtain relevant certifications. Implement regular security assessments and audits to ensure ongoing compliance with PCI-DSS requirements.

In conclusion, addressing security, privacy, and compliance considerations in cloud-based AI and machine learning environments requires a comprehensive approach that encompasses data security, model security, infrastructure security, and compliance with relevant regulations. By implementing appropriate security measures and ensuring compliance with regulations, organizations can mitigate risks, protect sensitive data, and build trust with users and stakeholders.

CHAPTER 10

FUTURE TRENDS AND DIRECTIONS

Exploring Emerging Trends and Advancements in AI, Machine Learning, and Cloud Computing

In recent years, the fields of artificial intelligence (AI), machine learning (ML), and cloud computing have witnessed significant advancements and transformative trends, paving the way for innovative solutions and new opportunities. Let's explore some of the emerging trends and advancements in these domains:

- AI and ML Automation: With the proliferation of data and the growing demand for AI and ML solutions, there is a trend towards automating various aspects of the AI and ML lifecycle. This includes automating data preprocessing, feature engineering, model selection, hyperparameter tuning, and deployment, thereby reducing the time and effort required to develop and deploy AI and ML solutions.

- Explainable AI (XAI): As AI and ML models become more complex and widespread, there is a growing need for transparency and interpretability in AI decision-making. Explainable AI (XAI) techniques aim to provide insights into how AI models arrive at their predictions or decisions, enabling stakeholders to understand, trust, and validate the outputs of AI systems.

- AI at the Edge: Edge computing, which involves processing data closer to the source or device, is gaining traction in AI and ML applications. By deploying AI models directly on edge devices such as sensors, cameras, and IoT devices, organizations can reduce latency, bandwidth usage, and reliance on centralized cloud infrastructure, while enabling real-time decision-making and insights at the edge.

- Federated Learning: Federated learning is a decentralized approach to training machine learning models across multiple devices or edge nodes while keeping the data localized. This enables organizations to leverage distributed data sources for model training without centralizing sensitive data in the cloud, thereby addressing privacy concerns and enabling collaboration in data-rich environments.

- AI Ethics and Responsible AI: With the increasing use of AI and ML in critical applications such as healthcare, finance, and criminal justice, there is growing awareness and concern about the ethical implications of AI technologies. Organizations and policymakers are focusing on developing ethical guidelines, standards, and regulations to ensure that AI systems are fair, transparent, accountable, and aligned with societal values.

- Quantum Computing: Quantum computing holds the promise of exponentially faster computation and the ability to solve complex problems that are currently intractable for classical computers. In the realm of AI and ML, quantum computing has the potential to accelerate tasks such as optimization, pattern recognition, and simulation, enabling breakthroughs in AI research and applications.

Predictions for the Future of AI and Machine Learning in the Cloud

Looking ahead, several trends and advancements are poised to shape the future of AI and machine learning in the cloud:

- Rise of Edge Computing: Edge computing will continue to gain prominence, enabling organizations to deploy AI and ML models closer to the data source for real-time processing, low-latency inference, and improved scalability.

- Federated Learning Adoption: Federated learning will become more widespread, allowing organizations to leverage distributed data sources for collaborative model training while addressing privacy, security, and regulatory concerns.

- Hybrid and Multi-cloud Deployments: Organizations will increasingly adopt hybrid and multi-cloud strategies, leveraging the strengths of different cloud providers and deployment models to optimize performance, cost, and flexibility for AI and ML workloads.

- AI-driven Automation: AI and ML technologies will play a central role in automating and optimizing various aspects of cloud computing, including resource provisioning, workload management, security, and cost optimization, leading to greater efficiency and agility in cloud environments.

- Integration of AI with DevOps and MLOps: The integration of AI with DevOps and MLOps practices will become standard practice, enabling organizations to streamline the development, deployment, and management of AI and ML applications in cloud environments.

- Advancements in Quantum Computing: Progress in quantum computing will accelerate, leading to breakthroughs in AI research and applications, including quantum machine learning algorithms, quantum neural networks, and quantum-enhanced optimization techniques.

Overall, the future of AI and machine learning in the cloud is characterized by innovation, collaboration, and transformation. By embracing emerging trends and advancements, organizations can unlock new opportunities, address complex challenges, and drive value creation in the digital era.

CONCLUSION

EMPOWERING THE FUTURE OF DATA: SUMMARY
AND KEY INSIGHTS

In the book "Empowering the Future of Data," we delve into the transformative potential of emerging technologies such as artificial intelligence (AI), machine learning (ML), and cloud computing in driving innovation and shaping the future of data science. Throughout the book, we explore the evolution of these technologies, their impact on various industries, and the opportunities they present for businesses and society as a whole.

One of the key insights from the book is the central role of data in today's digital economy. With the proliferation of connected devices, sensors, and digital platforms, organizations have access to vast amounts of data that can be leveraged to gain insights, make informed decisions, and create value. However, harnessing the full potential of data requires advanced technologies and capabilities, such as AI and ML, to analyze, interpret, and derive actionable insights from complex datasets.

Another key insight is the transformative impact of AI, ML, and cloud computing on traditional business models and processes. These technologies enable organizations to automate repetitive tasks, optimize operations, and drive innovation in areas such as product development, customer service, and marketing. By leveraging AI and ML algorithms, organizations can personalize customer experiences, improve predictive analytics, and optimize resource allocation, leading to increased efficiency, productivity, and competitiveness.

Furthermore, the book highlights the importance of ethical considerations and responsible use of data-driven technologies. As AI and ML become more pervasive in our daily lives, it's crucial for organizations to prioritize fairness, transparency, and accountability in their AI algorithms and decision-making processes. By adopting ethical AI principles and guidelines, organizations can build trust with customers, mitigate risks of bias and discrimination, and uphold the integrity of their data-driven initiatives.

In summary, "Empowering the Future of Data" provides a comprehensive overview of the transformative potential of AI, ML, and cloud computing in driving innovation and shaping the future of data science. By embracing these technologies, organizations can unlock new opportunities, solve complex challenges, and create value for customers, stakeholders, and society as a whole.

Reflections on the Transformative Potential of AI, Machine Learning, and Cloud Computing

As we reflect on the transformative potential of AI, machine learning, and cloud computing, it's clear that these technologies are reshaping the future of data science and driving innovation across various industries. From healthcare and finance to manufacturing and retail, organizations are leveraging AI and ML algorithms to unlock insights, optimize processes, and create new value propositions for customers.

One of the key transformative aspects of AI and ML is their ability to analyze and interpret vast amounts of data at scale, enabling organizations to make data-driven decisions and predictions with unprecedented accuracy and efficiency. Whether it's predicting customer behavior, optimizing supply chain operations, or diagnosing medical conditions, AI and ML algorithms have the potential to revolutionize how organizations operate and deliver value to their stakeholders.

Cloud computing plays a central role in enabling the scalability, flexibility, and accessibility of AI and ML technologies. By providing on-demand access to computing resources, storage, and platforms, cloud computing empowers organizations to deploy and scale AI and ML workloads rapidly, without the need for upfront investments in hardware or infrastructure. This democratization of computing power democratizes access to advanced analytics and data-driven insights, leveling the playing field for organizations of all sizes and industries.

However, as we embrace the transformative potential of AI, machine learning, and cloud computing, it's essential to recognize and address the ethical and societal implications of these technologies. Issues such as algorithmic bias, data privacy, and job displacement require careful consideration and proactive measures to ensure that AI-driven innovations benefit society as a whole. By prioritizing ethics, transparency, and responsible innovation, we can harness the full potential of AI, machine learning, and cloud computing to drive positive change and shape a future where data science empowers individuals, organizations, and communities alike.

In conclusion, AI, machine learning, and cloud computing have the power to transform how we collect, analyze, and leverage data to drive innovation and shape the future of data science. By embracing these technologies responsibly and ethically, we can unlock new opportunities, solve complex challenges, and create a brighter future for generations to come.

This book serves as a comprehensive guide for AI ML users, data scientists, machine learning engineers, software developers, and business leaders looking to harness the power of AI and machine learning in the cloud. By exploring the intersection of these technologies and providing practical insights and best practices, readers will gain the knowledge and skills needed to unlock the full potential of data science in the cloud era.

ABOUT AUTHOR

Anant Mittal

A nant Mittal is a Solutions Architect in Virginia. He is not merely a technical expert but a visionary leader who actively contributes to the advancement of society and the country at large. With a deep understanding of Cloud Computing, Artificial intelligence (AI) technologies and their potential applications, he plays a pivotal role in driving innovation, solving complex challenges, and creating value for individuals, organizations, and communities. He likes working on innovative solutions and is a passionate advocate for cloud computing technologies, promoting the benefits of scalability, flexibility and cost-efficiency that the cloud offers to businesses and organizations.

www.ingramcontent.com/pod-product-compliance
Lightning Source LLC
LaVergne TN
LVHW010040070326
832903LV00071B/4532